Help Me!
I'm All
Tied Up!

Binding and Loosing:
Scriptural Truth

Help Me! I'm All Tied Up!

All Scripture quotations are taken from the
Authorized King James Version of the Bible

Printed in the United States of America.
Cover photo created by Michelle Leivan

ISBN #1-58538-018-0

Leslie Johnson
Spirit of Prophecy Church
P. O. Box 750234
Topeka, KS   66675

e-mail at lesliej@cjnetworks.com
Phone: 785-266-1112

Table of Contents

Help Me! I'm All Tied Up!

Dedication

I want to thank You, Lord for bringing this revelation to me. You used one of your servants, Daniel Rodes, to open my eyes to spiritual truth. You definitely gave me *The Perfect Touch* when you revealed the mystery of binding and loosing.

My life has not been the same since. I pray that this information and knowledge will be the key many are looking for.

Thanks to you, Stan, my wonderful husband and my beautiful children for being patient and allowing me to spend many hours writing and putting this information on paper. Thank you Joyce, Jean and Michelle for doing the difficult task of editing my material. You are certainly a blessing from the Lord.

Help Me! I'm All Tied Up!

Introduction

Matthew 16:19 *And I will give unto thee the keys of the kingdom of heaven: and whatsoever thou shalt bind on earth shall be bound in heaven: and whatsoever thou shalt loose on earth shall be loosed in heaven.*

Matthew 18:18 *Verily I say unto you, Whatsoever ye shall bind on earth shall be bound in heaven: and whatsoever ye shall loose on earth shall be loosed in heaven.*

The Scriptures **Matthew 18:18** and **Matthew 16:19** have been verses that raised questions and have been misunderstood for as long as I can remember as a Christian.

Some become so dogmatic and religious about their interpretations of these Scriptures that they become unteachable and unbending. The purpose of this book is to help you unlock the mystery of binding and loosing.

Jesus says in the **Matthew 18:18** and **Matthew 16:19** that He will give us the keys of the kingdom of heaven. When you go to open a locked door, the key is what allows you to get in.

Sometimes while meditating on the Scriptures and with no revelation knowledge, the Lord will suddenly open your mind to understand them. It is like you try to unlock the door of the Scriptures over and over, but just cannot get it opened. All of a sudden, one day, the mystery (the door) is unlocked and you have understanding. This is what the Lord has done for me concerning binding and loosing.

He not only revealed the mystery of how to actually bind and loose, but also the mystery of the strong man. Too many times we listen to others teach the Word and never fully understand it. Many Christians certainly do not take the time to study the Word of God themselves.

During the many years I have prayed, I bound the devil and loosed the spirits of God in my life and for others. What I couldn't understand was that many times, although I had prayed with faith, the oppression would return. Sometimes there would be a temporary release, maybe even lasting for a season. I was plagued by persistent, gnawing questions. Why wasn't I completely free? Why wasn't the person I prayed for completely free? It seemed as though we were, but only for a short time.

It is very important to understand and internalize the Word of God. It is also important to see what Jesus did in similar situations. He was, and is our Example. Jesus is the One we are to follow.

This book will unlock the mystery of the keys to the kingdom of heaven. It will also help you comprehend the primary reasons for binding and loosing. The difference between binding and loosing will be explained. How Jesus prayed in these situations is revealed.

Another misconception concerns who the strong man really is as identified in the Word. This book will result in your having a clear understanding of the Scriptures and will enhance your prayer life because of the powerful truths contained herein. You will also recognize that curses and blessings are, for the most part, passed from one generation to the next.

Hopefully with revelation knowledge the Lord has imparted, to understanding these principles will change your life, as well as others you pray for.

There should be no confusion about or misunderstanding of God's Word. When there is, then dig deeper and pray more diligently. The Lord will be gracious to reveal His truth, which will set us free!

Chapter 1

To Bind or Not to Bind That Is the Question

Ephesians 4:29 *<u>Let no corrupt communication proceed out of your mouth</u>, but that which is good to the use of edifying, that it may minister grace unto the hearers.*

After I was baptized in the Holy Spirit in 1986, I began to be mentored by several Godly women. Their prayer life was magnificent, and I longed to be like them. They seemed to be so close to the Lord, and it always seemed like their prayers got answered. I would mimic the way that they prayed. These ladies were also mentored by others, and these mentors by someone else, and so forth.

I remember a time when I was with my spiritual mom, Mary Ellen, at a Bible study. All of a sudden, she stood up right in the middle of the teaching and began to come against Satan. The chalkboard kept falling off its pedestal, and she declared in a stern voice, "Satan, I bind you in the

Name of Jesus. I command you to leave, now!" Whoa, this was a bold woman and full of authority. I wanted that kind of boldness and authority. I didn't understand what she was doing, but it sounded right to me. She both bound and loosed Satan.

I had (and still have) such zeal for God and wanted so much to be used by Him. Because of this, I love to pray for people and see them free and healed of so many wounds, whether they be physical, emotional, financial, or spiritual.

One time in church a woman asked me to pray for her after the Sunday morning service. We had only been going to this particular church a couple of months, so I wasn't sure of the protocol. She exclaimed, "I have heard you pray and your prayers are answered! I want you to pray for me." I replied, "Okay, let's go up front to the altar, and I will pray for you there." "Well, I thought maybe we could go somewhere else," she responded. With what ultimately transpired, I'm so happy I insisted we pray at the altar. I took her up to the front near the altar and asked her, "What can I pray for you about?" "I have this lump on my neck, and I think it's cancer. I want to be healed," she answered.

I laid my hands on the side of her neck and began to pray as I had been taught. I bound Satan in the Name of Jesus and commanded that the cancerous spirit be removed and fall off of her. With this statement the woman (actually the demon inside her) put her hands around my neck, threw me on the floor, and began choking me to death. I was terrified and couldn't do or say anything. I remember thinking the Name of Jesus, but that was all I could do. Several church members were still in the sanctuary and they saw what was going on. Praise the Lord for His protection! They wrestled her off of me and began praying for her. The woman was finally set free—at least temporarily. I recount this experience to let you know that God gives us grace and mercy even in our ignorance, when we don't do things that line up with the Word of God.

The teaching I am about to bring you will be different for most of you. It will be a revelation to all of you. Once we know the truth about something, we are then responsible to follow through with what the Lord requires of us.

When I began to do a study on binding and loosing, I realized that I had not studied the Scriptures for myself. I had not discovered about how Jesus commanded evil spirits out. Once I did this, I recognized that I had been praying incorrectly for many years. However, through God's grace, He still healed and delivered many people through my intercession.

In summary, once we know a truth, we are then responsible to pray and act according to that revelation. **In other words, we are held accountable once we know the truth.**

> **Psalms 25:5** *Lead me in thy truth, and teach me: for thou art the God of my salvation; on thee do I wait all the day.*

> **John 8:32** *And ye shall know the truth, and the truth shall make you free.*

> **1 John 4:6** *We are of God: he that knoweth God heareth us; he that is not of God heareth not us. Hereby know we the spirit of truth, and the spirit of error.*

The Meaning Of Bind

First, let's find out what the word **bind** means. According to *Webster's Dictionary,* this word means to confine, restrain, or restrict as if with bonds. To bind means to put under obligation and constraint with legal authority. It also means to wrap or fasten around. When an opponent is bound, their freedom is restricted. It also means to hold, stick, secure, or tie together.

The Meaning Of Loose

What about the word **loose?** According to *Webster's Dictionary*, the word loose actually means to cast off; to free from obligation, responsibility, release, discharge, break up, destroy, or dissolve.

After much studying of **Matthew 16:19** where Jesus says, *"Whatsoever thou shalt bind on earth shall be bound in heaven and whatsoever thou shalt*

loose on earth shall be loosed in heaven," I have realized that throughout the Word of God, most teachings relate to either being bound or loosed. In otherwords, we are either in bondage to something or free. So many times we only pay attention to the words bind and loose in this Scripture.

The Key to Opening the Scripture?

In the first part of **Matthew 16:19**, Jesus says, *"I will give you the keys of the kingdom of heaven."* What keys are being referred to by the Lord? I believe the keys lead us to recognize that our whole life in the Lord is characterized by one of two conditions: Either we are free from sin or we are bound up in sin. Some examples would be, "That just tickles me to death!" "My feet are killing me!" "You're bad." "You're an accident waiting to happen!" You can probably think of many more statements we make that curse, and therefore bind, others or ourselves. We can bind and loose ourselves and others through the words we speak.

Only Jesus can forgive our sins. We doom ourselves many times by being hypocrites. **We can either absolve or retain sins.** If we are bound by sin on this earth, we will be in heaven, and if we are loosed from sin on this earth, we will also be in heaven. This is a good thing. Once we are freed from bondage, we can enjoy being joint heirs with Christ.

Throughout the Word of God, the Lord is dealing with binding and loosing. He gives parable after parable that illustrates either being tied up or freed. We can either be free from bondage or loosed from it.

Matthew 16:19 and other verses dealing with the subject, e.g. Matthew 18:18, aren't talking about binding and loosing the devil, but instead telling us we have the authority either to keep ourselves bound or free. If you bind yourself with words of death, then you are bound on earth as well as in heaven. Are you bound with unforgiveness, or have you repented and become free? You should loose unforgiveness off your life right now and be free. Are we going to forbid bondage to dominate our lives or allow it?

Everyone is servant to some master. When a person is commanded to do something, they yield to the master's command. Everyone yields...for instance whether to a sinful disposition of the heart or a disposition toward obedience. One is a willing slave to sin. Again we who are servants of Jesus Christ were once slaves of sin, but now are joint heirs with Jesus.

> **Romans 6:19** *I speak after the manner of men because of the infirmity of your flesh: for as ye have yielded your members servants to uncleanness and to iniquity unto iniquity; even so now yield your members servants to righteousness unto holiness.*

In my study of binding and loosing, I found 49 Scriptures that contain the word bind, 29 Scriptures that have the word loose, and 474 Scripture references with the word cast. [If a dog is tied to a tree, he is bound. Not until he is untied is he loosed from that tree.] In **Proverbs 3:3** the Lord instructs us to not forsake mercy and truth. He further goes on to command us to bind them about our necks and write them upon the tables of our hearts.

> **Proverbs 3:3** *Let not mercy and truth forsake thee: bind them about thy neck; write them upon the table of thine heart:*

This Scripture is describing an attitude of your heart. If you desire the truth of God's Word, then you love truth. You also recognize the Lord's mercy to us. These are important character traits, such as love and faithfulness. Someone with this type of character will demonstrate it by their actions.

Think about a loving person you know. This person not only feels love, but he or she also acts upon this emotion. They are loyal and responsible. You can trust them. What about a faithful person? Are they faithful in their actions? A faithful person usually works to help others be faithful as well. Just believing that you are faithful, loving, merciful, and searching for truth is not enough. Your actions must align with your attitudes.

Another Scripture about binding is found in **Isaiah 8:16**.

Isaiah 8:16 *Bind up the testimony, seal the law among my disciples.*

To "bind up the testimony" and "seal the law" actually means the Words of God were to be written down and preserved for future generations. As God's children, we have the responsibility of passing on the Word of God to our children, grandchildren, and so on...generation after generation. We need to encourage our heritage to love the Bible, read and internalize its contents, and then act accordingly. As we do our part, the generations that follow will be faithful in raising their children in the nurture and admonition of the Lord.

> **Ephesians 6:4** *And, ye fathers, provoke not your children to wrath: but bring them up in the nurture and admonition of the Lord.*

What Did Jesus Do?

Nowhere in the Scriptures did I find that Jesus ever bound a demon, Lucifer, Satan, the devil, or any demonic principalities and rulers of darkness. You might object, "What about in **Isaiah 61:1** where it says, *"He hath sent me to bind up the brokenhearted..."*

> **Isaiah 61:1** *The Spirit of the Lord GOD is upon me; because the LORD hath anointed me to preach good tidings unto the meek; <u>he hath sent me to bind up the brokenhearted</u>, to proclaim liberty to the captives, and the opening of the prison to them that are bound;*

The word bind in this Scripture actually means to compress or medicate. The *Strong's Concordance* reference number 2280 is "Chabash." Chabash means to wrap firmly, compress, medicate, or to stop the hurt. This Scripture isn't telling us to bind Satan or his evil powers and authorities. We are to heal, soothe, and comfort the brokenhearted.

We believers in Jesus Christ and those who don't believe in Jesus must live side-by-side in this world. God allows unbelievers to remain for awhile, just as a farmer allows weeds to remain in his field for a time. According to a farmer friend of mine, the reason a farmer allows weeds to remain in his field for a time is so the surrounding wheat isn't uprooted with them when they are pulled, but at the time of harvest, the weeds are uprooted.

Is it Harvesting Time Yet?

Matthew 13:30 *<u>Let both grow together until the harvest</u>: and in the time of harvest I will say to the reapers, Gather ye together first the tares, and bind them in bundles to burn them: but gather the wheat into my barn.*

The **tares are what are bound up.** At the time of the end, God will uproot the evil and throw them away to be burned. We need to continue seeking righteousness and holiness and making ourselves ready at all times to go home to be with the Lord. Make sure your faith is sincere and demonstrated by your works. Also, notice that Jesus tells the reapers to gather the tares first. The reapers are angels. At the time of Jesus' return, He will send out His reapers, the angels, to gather the tares, (the wicked) and then the wheat (the believers). That does away with the pre-tribulation theory, doesn't it?

Where Do I Send the Demons?

Jesus didn't bind demons, He only cast them out. Then where did He send them once He had cast them out? As you study the Scriptures, you will find that, *Jesus didn't send them anywhere. He only cast them out and commanded them to go.* You say, "But Leslie, Jesus sent them to outer darkness according to **Matthew 22:13**, right?"

Matthew 22:13 *Then said the king to the servants, Bind him hand and foot, and take him away, and <u>cast him into</u>*

*__outer darkness__, there shall be weeping and gnashing of
teeth.*

As we look at this chapter in context, in **Matthew 22:8** Jesus spoke to His
servants and said that the wedding is ready. **The wedding feast with our
Lord is not until the end,** just as the time of the harvest is at the end. It is
not until Jesus' return that all the evil spirits of darkness in this world and in
the heavenlies, and those people without wedding garments, are sent into outer
darkness. This Scripture is written in the future tense showing us what Jesus
will do.

Jesus didn't have the authority in His earthly incarnation, nor do we, to
bind Satan and cast him into outer darkness, because the time of the end is not
yet. We are not yet at the time of the harvest.

In **Matthew 25:30**, the Lord will, at the time of the end, cast the un-
profitable servant into outer darkness. This man was only thinking of himself.
He buried his money and thought he would get away with it. This wicked and
slothful man was hoping to protect himself, but he was judged for his self-
centeredness. Many times, as Christians, we make excuses to avoid doing what
God calls us to do. If Jesus is really our Master, we <u>must</u> obey Him. Our time,
abilities, and money aren't ours in the first place. We are only the caretakers—
not the owners. If we ignore, squander, or abuse what we are given, then we are
rebellious and deserve to be punished. As we pray and ask for blessings from
the Lord, do you think He will give us more if we aren't taking care of what He
has already placed in our hands ?

Jesus commanded the demons to loose their hold. He cast them out. We
are to do the same. We don't have the authority to send them to outer darkness, to hell, to the pit, to the ground or anywhere else. Our job is to take
authority over the demons like Jesus did and command them to loose their
hold and come out. Nowhere in Scripture does it tell us where to send the
demons. The Lord simply says to resist the devil and he shall flee.

The devil is seeking whom he can devour. He comes to steal, kill and
destroy.

1 Peter 5:8 *Be sober, be vigilant; because your adversary the devil, as a roaring lion, walketh about, <u>seeking whom he may devour:</u>*

Are you available for the enemy to devour? The Word says <u>he is seeking whom he can.</u> Don't become available. As believers, we already have the victory. Many times, because of our rebellious natures we get all tied up in knots and fall prey to the enemy.

I have had people say to me, "Leslie, if I pray for someone else and I cast the demon out of them, I'm afraid that the demon will attack me if I don't tie them up or send them somewhere. What if the demon comes back on me or someone near me?"

How to Cast Out Demons

1. First, let's remember the Scriptures. Jesus is our example of how to cast out devils. If we are to pray as He did, then we don't need to add anything.

2. Secondly, if you are afraid of a demon attacking you, then you don't have the right to be praying for someone anyway. We are not to fear demons—**they are to fear us.**

3. Finally, before praying for anyone, you yourself should be free of sin and cleansed from all unrighteousness

1 John 1:9 *If we confess our sins, he is faithful and just to forgive us our sins, and to cleanse us from all unrighteousness.*

You should already have the full armor of God on, the Blood of Jesus covering you, and the Lord's ministering and guardian angels placed about you.

Even if we could send the demons somewhere else, they wouldn't stay where we send them, because Satan is the prince of the air. A third of the fallen angels are either running rampant on the earth or in the atmosphere.

What about **Matthew 8:31-32** where Jesus sent the devils into the swine?

Matthew 8:31-32 *So the devils besought him, saying, If thou cast us out, suffer us to go away into the herd of swine. And he said unto them, Go. And when they were come out, they went into the herd of swine: and, behold, the whole herd of swine ran violently down a steep place into the sea, and perished in the waters.*

The devils asked Jesus to please send them to the swine. This was the only Scripture reference that Jesus sent a demon anywhere. However, notice they asked and He allowed it.

In **Luke 13:12**, Jesus said to the woman with the spirit of infirmity, "...*thou are **loosed** from thine infirmity.*" If you want to bind anything, I hope you see in the Word that you **only bind the good**. Does it make sense to tie a demon onto a person? No! Does it make sense to loose the demon off a person? Yes!

Scriptures indicate that we bind the good spirits of God to a person. We also are to loose the evil spirits of fallen angels off the person, telling them to **"Go!" For example, if someone has a haughty (prideful) spirit, you would loose off the haughty spirit and you would bind the contrite, humble Spirit of God to them**. Another example would be if someone has a spirit of error on them, you would **loose the spirit of error off of them and bind the spirit of truth to them**.

You must, however, realize that until someone really wants to be free we can pray for them, but they won't be delivered until they make the decision by exercising their free will.

There are 499 verses containing the word spirit or spirits in the Bible. As you study the different verses you will begin to see the spirits of God and the spirits of the devil.

Proverbs 17:27 *He that hath knowledge spareth his words: and a man of understanding is of an excellent spirit.*

An excellent spirit is of God. If someone has a perverse or foul spirit, this would be of Satan. Therefore, in this situation you would **bind the excellent spirit of God to the person and loose the foul, ungodly spirit of perversion off them.**

Another example is the jealous spirit. This evil spirit especially loves to take root in families. If you have had sex before marriage or committed adultery, a jealous spirit will enter into the marriage and home. The same goes for masturbation, since this is a form of fornication.

A jealous spirit can be manifested in many different ways. If someone in a family has committed a sexual crime and not repented of the evil, ungodly soul tie that formed as a result; a lot of anger, rage, hatred, revenge, strife, envy, selfishness, and even murder can and will enter the home. Watch the news reports when adultery has been committed and the terrible things the partners do to each other afterward. Remember John Wayne Bobbit? O. J. Simpson?

The "secret" sin of masturbation in a household will result in anger and hatred in the home. Do you find that you are a happy person and then you walk in the door of your home and anger just leaps on you? Jesus knows all of our secret sins. Masturbation is a sin many don't recognize as a sexual sin.

How do we get rid of the spirit of jealousy? It takes repentance and walking it out with God's grace. Once repentance has taken place, the person praying over you would **bind the spirit of the love of God and loose the spirit of jealousy.**

19

Soul Ties

What is an ungodly soul tie? The soul tie is created between you and anyone whom we have had sexual intercourse with or even have engaged in heavy petting with. This also includes oral or anal sex. It doesn't matter whether or not you were sexually aroused. If this has occurred with anyone outside of marriage, then you have an ungodly soul tie with that person.

Men and women, if you have had sexual fantasies about another person, you have an ungodly soul tie with them. When you commit the sin of masturbation while watching a pornographic movie, looking at a dirty magazine, fantasizing about someone, you have an ungodly soul tie with the other persons depicted.

What about abortion? You have created an ungodly soul tie with whoever takes the baby from your womb. Obviously any kind of molestation, sexual perversion, and sexual sin committed against someone causes an ungodly soul tie to be created. Even if the sin was perpetrated against you, there is an ungodly soul tie that needs to be broken.

Is it Important to Break the Soul Ties?

It is important to break the soul tie because when two people have sex, even by masturbation while looking at a magazine or film, the two become one. Just as married couples become one flesh the night of consummation of their love, the same is true whenever the sexual act takes place. You take that person to bed with you each and every night until you break the tie. The sin has not been removed from your spirit until you take action to remove the sin in the Name of Jesus.

What Do I Do to Break this Filthy Tie?

First, renounce all sexual sin with another. Name the names of persons you have had sexual encounters with out loud. If it was a film or magazine, speak it out loud and renounce the sin. Command the ungodly soul tie to be severed and broken. Command in the Name of Jesus that there will be no longer be an ungodly soul tie bound to your body, soul, or spirit. Ask forgiveness, and forgive those who may have harmed and hurt you. Declare that any ungodly soul ties from past generations be broken, severed, and removed from you from the very first thought, word, gesture, or deed. Command these ungodly soul ties to be severed from the tenth generation or as far back as need be. As a result, the generation now and those to come will be free from all ungodly soul ties in the Name of Jesus. Hallelujah!

Mark 9:25 *When Jesus saw that the people came running together, he rebuked the foul spirit, saying unto him, Thou* <u>*dumb and deaf spirit,*</u> *I charge thee,* <u>*come out of him,*</u> *and enter no more into him.*

Romans 8:15 *For ye have not received the spirit of bondage again to fear; but ye have received the Spirit of adoption, whereby we cry, Abba, Father.*

Romans 8:15 is clear about what to bind and what to loose. If you are in bondage to fear, then you would **loose the spirit of fear and bind the spirit of adoption.**

Remember, we are not to fear but instead have power, love, and a sound mind.

2 Timothy 1:7 *For God hath not given us the spirit of fear; but of power, and of love, and of a sound mind.*

The way to have this freedom is to stay in the Word of God and meditate. Desire to be free, and the Lord will set you free. Stay teachable, and earnestly desire the gifts of the Holy Spirit.

Chapter 2

Evil Spirits

The following evil spirits are to be loosed off people. You never bind them to anyone!

1. The spirit of Anti-Christ (1 John 4:3) Isaiah Chapters 13 and 14; & 2 Thessalonians 2:4

This spirit is what it says, against-Christ. Also, this spirit wants to take the place of Christ. Anyone who opposes the deity of Christ has this spirit. Someone who blasphemes and comes against Christians has this spirit. Someone who is of the world and not of God has this spirit. Anyone who denies Jesus is Lord has this spirit. Other manifestations of the spirit of anti-christ include lawlessness. Lawlessness means obviously without law. Someone with this sin is denying the authority of God. Other manifestations of this spirit are: New Age beliefs and humanism, worship of mother earth, persecution of the children of the Lord, and denial of the gifts of the Holy Spirit.

<u>Bind the *Spirit of the Lord* and *excellent spirit* to this person. Also, you could bind the *spirit of truth*. Loose *the spirit*</u>

23

of anti-Christ, in the Name of Jesus.

2. The spirit of bondage (Romans 8:15)

The spirit of bondage is being a slave to something. This spirit includes any kind of fear or anxiety. The spirit of bondage afflicts anyone with mental or psychological disorders. Other manifestations of this spirit include pornography, greed or any kind of addiction.

Bind the _spirit of adoption_. Loose _the spirit of bondage_ in the Name of Jesus.

3. The spirit of fear (Romans 8:15 & 2 Timothy 1:7)

The spirit of fear includes any kind of fear or phobia, anxiety, terror, dread, trembling and oppression, depression, shyness, and self-centeredness.

Bind the _spirit of wisdom_. Also the perfect love casteth out all fear. The perfect love is Jesus Christ; therefore, bind the _spirit of the Lord_. Loose _the spirit of fear_. Command it to go, in the Name of Jesus.

4. Anguish of spirit (Exodus 6:9)

This spirit is associated with heartbreak, distress, misery, suffering, grief, and torment.

Put on the _garment of praise_. Also, bind the _spirit of wisdom and the fruit of the spirit_. Loose _the spirit of anguish_ off in the Name of Jesus.

5. Unclean spirit (Mark 5:8)

Manifestations of this spirit include someone who is defiled or has defiled someone or something. These would include something or someone contaminated, filthy, foul-mouthed, sloppy, evil, profane, impure, and corrupted.

> **Bind the *spirit of wisdom, an excellent spirit, and a spirit of Holiness*. Loose *the unclean spirit* in the Name of Jesus.**

6. The spirit of Divination (Acts 16:16-18)

Manifestations encountered with this spirit include psychic ability and any kind of witchcraft. Someone who is rebellious, stubborn, uses drugs, and is in any way associated with the occult or New Age has this spirit. A hypnotist works by the spirit of divination.

> **Bind a *spirit of wisdom, truth and holiness*. Loose *the spirit of divination* in the Name of Jesus.**

7. A familiar spirit (2 Kings 21:6)

This spirit works with the spirit of divination. Psychics, and anyone using the evil spirits to obtain information instead of the Holy Spirit, have a familiar spirit.

> **Bind the *Holy Spirit*. Command the *familiar spirit* to go in the Name of Jesus.**

8. The dumb and deaf spirit (Mark 9:25-26)

Some manifestations of the dumb and deaf spirit include foaming at the mouth, a foul spirit, suicidal thoughts or tendencies, ear problems, deafness, and the paranoid mental illnesses. A dumb and deaf spirit will cause people to be distracted and not pay attention. Grinding of teeth, blindness and drowning are other manifestations of this spirit.

> **Bind the *spirit of wisdom*. Also the *fruit of the spirit*, and the *spirit of faith*. Cast out the *dumb and deaf spirit* in the Name of Jesus.**

9. A foul spirit (Mark 9:25)

A foul spirit is an abomination to the Lord. Its manifestations include hate, offensiveness, viciousness, wickedness, blasphemy, a foul mouth, indecency, obscenity, unscrupulousness, and desecration.

> **Command the *foul unclean spirit* to leave and bind *the excellent spirit of God* in the Name of Jesus.**

Some spirits are crossed over from one to the other. Many manifestations are the same.

10. A spirit of heaviness (Isaiah 61:3)

Discouragement, self pity, a complaining spirit, and rejection are only a few of this spirit's manifestations. Someone who is severely depressed and has spells of uncontrollable crying has this spirit. Other manifestations are feelings of loneliness, despair, and hopelessness. If this spirit is on someone, they have a difficult time forgiving. Asthma and other breathing difficulties are because of this spirit's presence.

> **Put on the *garment of praise* for the *spirit of heaviness* and bind the *spirit of wisdom*. Command the *spirit of heaviness* to go in the Name of Jesus.**

11. A haughty spirit (Proverbs 16:18)

Pride and arrogance characterize the haughty spirit. Other manifestations include dominance and dictatorship. Someone who is stiffnecked, stubborn, and hard-headed has a haughty spirit.

> **Bind the *contrite and humble spirit*. Loose *the haughty spirit* from the person and command the spirit to bow to the Name of Jesus.**

12. A prideful spirit (Proverbs 29:23)

Manifestations of this spirit include those who flatter themselves; being overbearing, boastful, egotistical, cocky, self-loving, self-glorifying, overconfident and puffed up.

> **Bind the *contrite and humble spirit*. Command the *prideful spirit* to bow in the Name of Jesus.**

13. The spirit of infirmity (Luke 13:11)

Manifestations of this spirit include impotency, blindness, fever, and all types of sickness and disease, as well as any kind of crippling, lameness, and palsy. The spirit of heaviness often accompanies with this spirit.

> **Bind the _spirit of faith and wisdom._ Loose the _spirit of infirmity_ and command it to go in the Name of Jesus.**

14. A spirit of jealousy (Numbers 5:14, 30)

This is one of the hardest spirits to rid oneself of. The manifestations include rage, hatred, strife, anger, revenge, selfishness, envy and division. The most common way for a spirit of jealousy to enter is due to a person committing adultery or any kind of sexual perversion.

> **Bind the _spirit of truth and holiness,_ and for the _fruit of the Spirit_ to be evident in the person's life. Command the _spirit of jealousy_ and all its manifestations to leave in the Name of Jesus.**

15. The spirit of error (1 John 4:6)

Manifestations of this spirit include someone who is a victim of delusion, inaccuracy, fallacy, misbelief, oversight, misconception, and absurdity.

> **Bind the _spirit of truth._ Command the _spirit of error_ to leave in the Name of Jesus.**

16. A lying spirit (2 Chronicles 18:22)

Someone who exaggerates operates with this spirit in their life. Other manifestations include lies, deception, a religious spirit, denial, gossip, profanity, and slander. Also included would be superstitions and not being reliable.

Bind the _spirit of truth_. Also the _Holy Spirit and the spirit of excellence_. Loose the _lying spirit_ and command it to cease in the Name of Jesus.

17. A perverse spirit (Isaiah 19:14)

This spirit perverts God's Word. Also a wounded spirit is evident when this spirit is present. Other manifestations would include all sexual sins, e.g., homosexuality, lesbianism, incest, prostitution, and involvement in pornography. A person with a perverted spirit is operating in a spirit of error. They are consumed with lust and perverted sexual thoughts including anal sex, oral sex, and sex with animals. They are a lover of themselves and a hater of God.

Bind the _spirit of wisdom and truth_. Command the _foul and perverted, lying spirit_ to go in the Name of Jesus.

18. The spirit of whoredoms (Hosea 5:4)

Manifestations of this spirit would include idolatry, adultery, fornication, prostitution, love of the world, and eating disorders, love of money, and any type of addiction.

Bind the _spirit of adoption, the spirit of truth, and the Holy Spirit_. Loose _the spirit of whoredoms_ in the Name of Jesus.

Dealing With Generational Curses

Evil spirits bearing generational curses are mentioned in the Bible. These evil, foul spirits have many different manifestations. Many times people are plagued by sickness, disease, palsy, or degenerative diseases because of curses passed down from previous generations. We can also invite these spirits in ourselves. We need to also remember that some infirmities and diseases aren't removed by binding and loosing. This can be difficult to understand, but God's ways are higher than our's. I do know that Jesus came and bore all our sickness and disease in His body on the cross. We need to continue to pray for our sisters and brothers, exercising our faith that they _will_ be set free.

Before praying, always remember to ask forgiveness for your sins and the sins of your forefathers. Put on the full armor of God, and plead the blood of Jesus over yourself and the person you are ministering to. This is cleansing. Also, don't forget to pray that you will have the ministering, guardian, and all angels of the Lord surrounding you and your family.

Remember one more thing. Some spirits do not come out except first by fasting.

Matthew 17:21 _Howbeit this kind goeth not out but by prayer and fasting._

Pray, seek, and ask the Lord's direction and that He might use you as a willing vessel whom He can work through.

Chapter 3

Spirits of God

The following spirits are to be bound to a person. As you loose the evil spirits off the person, then bind a spirit of God to them.

1. The Spirit of the Lord (Judges 3:10)

Obviously, if someone has an *anti-Christ* spirit then you would **bind the *Spirit of the Lord to them*. Loose the *spirit of fear* in the Name of Jesus.**

2. The Spirit of wisdom (Exodus 31:3)

Characteristics of this spirit include clear thinking, mental and emotional balance, good judgment, discernment, knowledge, prudence, sanity, and stability.

Loose a *spirit of fear, dumb and deaf spirit, a spirit of*

heaviness, spirit of divination, a spirit of infirmity, and a perverted and unclean spirit. __Bind the *spirit of wisdom* in the Name of Jesus.__

3. An *excellent* spirit (Proverbs 17:27)

A person manifesting this spirit would be admirable, distinctive, good, great, skillful, notable and exceptional.

After you loosed a *spirit of fear, a lying spirit, and unclean spirit;* you would __bind the *excellent spirit*__ to someone.

4. The spirit of *truth* (John 14:17)

This spirit of God includes such things as honesty, precision, authenticity, credibility and dependability.

You would __bind the *spirit of Truth*__ if someone has __an *anti-Christ spirit, a spirit of heaviness, a spirit of jealousy, a lying and perverted spirit, the spirit of error, and the spirit of whoredom.*__

5. The Holy Spirit (Ephesians 1:13)

The Nine Gifts of the Holy Spirit

1 Corinthians 12:8-10 *For to one is given by the Spirit the word of __wisdom__; to another the word of __knowledge__ by the same spirit; To another __faith__ by the same Spirit; to another* *the gifts of <u>healing</u> by the same Spirit; To another the <u>working of miracles</u>; to another <u>prophecy</u>; to another <u>discerning of spirits</u>; to another <u>divers kinds of tongues</u>; to another the <u>interpretation of tongues</u>:*

You would **bind** *the Holy Spirit* to someone if they have a *spirit of divination, a lying or familiar spirit, or a spirit of whoredoms.*

6. The fruit of the Spirit (Galatians 5:23-24)

power, love, and sound mind (2 Timothy 1:7).

Bind the *fruit of the Spirit* if someone has been loosed from the *spirit of fear, heaviness, jealousy, or the dumb and deaf spirit.*

7. A contrite and humble spirit (Isaiah 57:15)

If someone has a *haughty or prideful spirit*, you would loose those spirits and *bind the contrite and humble spirit to them.*

The characteristics of someone with a contrite and humble spirit are apologetic, chastened, remorseful, and sorrowful. They are also content, courteous, gentle, mild, modest, polite, and unobtrusive.

If someone is obnoxious and loud, **loose the** *haughty spirit* **and bind the** *contrite and humble Spirit of God* **to them in the Name of Jesus.**

8. The spirit of holiness (Romans 1:4)

Holiness means to have faith, grace, humility, reverence, righteousness, and to be devout, Godly, and virtuous.

You would **bind the *spirit of holiness*** to someone who has the *spirit of divination, a spirit of perversion, an unclean spirit, a spirit of jealousy or the spirit of anti-Christ.*

9. A spirit of faith (2 Corinthians 4:13)

Faith is total trust in someone. Other characteristics of faith include acceptance, allegiance, assurance, belief, confidence, conviction, dependence, hope, loyalty, sureness, and worship.

Bind the *spirit of faith* if the *spirit of fear, heaviness, infirmity, or the dumb and deaf spirit* have been loosed.

10. The spirit of Glory (1 Peter 4:14)

When someone has the spirit of glory, there is evidence of dignity and honor in their life. They will have a good reputation and be triumphant.

Loose the *spirit of divination* and **bind the *spirit of glory* in the Name of Jesus.**

11. The garment of praise for the spirit of heaviness (Isaiah 61:3)

Someone wearing the garment of praise will approve, bless, dignify, honor, proclaim, reverence, smile, and worship.

Loose the *spirits of fear, heaviness, bondage and the dumb and deaf spirit* in the Name of Jesus. <u>Bind the *garment of praise* to them</u>.

12. The spirit of prophecy (Revelation 19:10)

Revelation 19:10 *And I fell at his feet to worship him. And he said unto me, See thou do it not: I am thy fellowservant, and of thy brethren that have the testimony of Jesus: worship God: for the testimony of Jesus is the spirit of prophecy.*

<u>Loose the *spirit of divination and the anti-Christ spirit* in</u> the Name of Jesus, and <u>bind the *spirit of prophecy*.</u>

13. The spirit of adoption (Romans 8:15)

If someone is adopted in the Lord, they will experience acceptance and approval. They will feel embraced, supported, raised, and nurtured.

Loose the *spirit of bondage and whoredoms* in the Name of Jesus. <u>Bind the *spirit of adoption*.</u>

Remember, Jesus is our example. He commissioned us to heal the sick, cleanse the lepers, raise the dead, and cast out devils. The only way we can truly accomplish these assignments is to be cleansed ourselves. Perfect love casts out all fear. Don't allow fear to keep you from fulfilling the Lord's plan for your life.

We don't need to fear demons–they need to fear us. We are disciples of

Christ. We don't need to fear anything or any person. The only One we fear, and it is a reverential fear, is the Lord Jesus.

Someone needs to desire to be cleansed to fully receive deliverance. We can pray and intercede, but it isn't until the person desires freedom that they will truly be free.

Matthew 10:1 *And when he had called unto him his twelve disciples, he gave them power against unclean spirits, to cast them out, and to heal all manner of sickness and all manner of disease.*

Chapter 4

Understanding the Strong Man

Mark 3:27 *No man can enter into a strong man's house, and spoil his goods, except he will first bind the strong man; and then he will spoil his house.*

What is the strong man? First of all, well and good meaning people put the two words together instead of separating strong and man as it is in Scripture. There is a misconception that the "strongman" is actually a demonic force that has a hold over a person. Even those who teach "bind the good", and "loose the evil" still try to justify this interpretation. We can examine Mark 3:27, we find that this interpretation ("strongman") would be contrary to the true meaning of what to bind and what to loose. Since Jesus is our example, then we need to realize that according to Scripture, He never bound demons. Obviously there is more to this verse than we assume.

The Strong Man's House

As we read **Mark 3:27**, sentence by sentence, the first part says that no man can enter into a strong man's house. Who is the no man and who is the strong man? **Mark 3:25** tells us, *"If a house be divided against itself, then that house cannot stand."* **Verse 26** says, *"If Satan rises up against himself, and be divided, he could not stand."* In other words, Satan won't cast out Satan, will he?

In the *Strong's Concordance* when it says "no man," this means that nothing, no one will be able to have the power, even the thoughts that come into the mind will not be able to enter the strong man's house.

A strong man according to the concordance is someone strong in body, mind, and one who has the <u>strength of soul to sustain the attacks of Satan.</u> Huh? You mean the strong man is not demonic in nature? Not according to the Word of God. How could Satan attack Satan?

Who Lives in the House?

What is the house? The house is an inhabited place, a dwelling, property, wealth, or goods. So let's put this in perspective. According to the Word, Jesus says no man, which means nothing, no one can enter into a strong man's house. If Satan cannot enter the strong man's house, then the strong man must be you and me. If we are saved, are strong in body and mind, and have the strength to overcome Satan, then we must be the strong man.

The Scripture says, *"No man can enter into a strong man's house and spoil his goods, except he will first bind the strong man and then he will spoil his house."*

Spoil Whose Goods?

What are our goods? Our goods include our body (the temple of the Holy Spirit), where we dwell (our property), wealth, etc. The only way that Satan can spoil our goods is if he comes in and puts us in bondage and binds, or ties us up. If he binds us up, then he, Satan, can spoil our house.

Now, let's see what Scripture is really saying here.

> **Mark 3:25-27** *And if a house be divided against itself, that house cannot stand. And if Satan rise up against himself, and be divided, he cannot stand, but hath an end. No man [Nothing, no one, will be able or have the power, even the thoughts that come into the mind.] can enter into a strong man's [Someone strong in body, mind, one who has the strength to sustain the attacks of Satan, and is strong] house [inhabited place, dwelling, property, wealth, goods], and spoil his goods, except he will first bind [tie up, fasten, Satan taking possession, bind up] the strong man; [One who has strength of soul to sustain the attacks of Satan.] and then he [Satan] will spoil his house.*

How Can Satan Enter Our Home?

How can Satan enter our dwelling? I believe the main route is through fear. If we allow different fears to enter our mind and act on them, then Satan has a stronghold in our life. The only way that Satan can put us in bondage and spoil our house is if we give him the opening. The way we give openings to the devil is through rebellion and sin. If we don't repent and stay in obedience, we give him an open door to enter.

In the Garden of Eden when Adam and Eve sinned, fear is the first thing that took root in them. Many times scholars have believed that shame and guilt was upon them. This is also true, but when they heard the voice of the Lord in the Garden, the first reaction and manifestation of the sin they committed was fear.

> **Genesis 3:10** *And he said, I heard thy voice in the garden, and I was afraid, because I was naked; and I hid myself.*

Think about Adam and Eve for a moment. Could Adam have reacted in fear before Eve ate of the tree? The Word tells us that God gave Adam a command. God said to Adam, "Thou shalt not eat of it." The Lord never said, "Thou shalt not touch the tree of knowledge." I believe that Adam loved Eve so much and wanted to protect her so diligently that he wanted to make sure she didn't get near that tree. Did Adam open a door through this fear for the subtle beast of the field to tempt? What did God tell Adam?

Genesis 2:17 ***But of the tree of the knowledge of good and evil, thou shalt not eat of it: for in the day that thou eatest thereof thou shalt surely die.***

The Fall of Man

Genesis 3:1-3 *Now the serpent was more subtil than any beast of the field which the LORD God had made. And he said unto the woman, Yea, hath God said, Ye shall not eat of every tree of the garden? And the woman said unto the serpent, We may eat of the fruit of the trees of the garden: But of the fruit of the tree which is in the midst of the garden, **God hath said, Ye shall not eat of it, neither shall ye touch it, lest ye die.***

Where did Eve come up with "Ye shall not eat of it, neither shall ye touch it, lest ye die?" What did Adam tell Eve? Could it be that fear entered the scene even in the Garden? Our greatest attack from Satan has and always will be fear. If we succumb to an attack of Satan with any kind of fear, then he has us!

In **Luke 11**, Jesus tells us about the strong man. If a strong man is armed and keeps his palace, then his goods are in peace. With the teaching that the strong man is a demon, how is he armed? Most importantly, t**he demon doesn't own the temple of the Holy Spirit.** Our body is His temple. Not only that, a demon would not be in peace.

Stay Strong and Armed

How do Christians stay armed? The first way is through prayer - daily prayer when you put on the full armor of God. The sword of the spirit, which is the Word of God, is your offensive weapon. Keep the joy of the Lord, which is your strength, and you will also keep your peace.

In **Luke 11:22**, Jesus talks about when one stronger than he (the strong man) shall come upon him and overcome him, then the armor is taken from the man and Satan divides his spoils. Who is one "stronger than he"? This is an evil spirit that is able to overcome us when we sin because of yielding to temptation. However, remember we are overcomers by the Blood of the Lamb and the word of our testimony (the Word of God).

When an unclean spirit is gone out of man, the Scriptures tell us that it seeks rest and cannot find it. The evil spirit decides to enter the house (the person) that it came out of. When the evil spirit returns to this house and finds it swept and garnished, Jesus tells us it takes seven other spirits more wicked than itself to dwell there also.

How can the evil spirit re-enter if the person is clean? We find the reason in the Scriptures. If the area from which the demon departed isn't replaced with the Word of God and the person keeping the Word, then the door is opened wide. If a person wants to stay bound up, they will! How? They will reopen the door to the evil spirits, and they will be worse off than before. A person must desire, confess, and believe that they truly want to be set free.

Have you ever met a Christian who lives in despair continuously? They live in self-pity and depression with a "woe is me" attitude. It seems that no matter what you do, say, or even pray, they will not be free. Someone might have an illness. They use this as a crutch to get sympathy and attention. Oh, they come up every Sunday for prayer and say that they want to be healed. They may even get slain in the Spirit, but they get up and a short time later they are back where they were before complaining and murmuring. Unfortunately, these people have become comfortable with the demon that possesses them. They don't want to be free of the devil. They would rather stay in the state they're in rather than be free. Only they can really determine whether they want to be free or stay in bondage. I would like to state a word of caution here. Just because someone is not healed does not mean they have a demon. I have seen too many times in the Christian arena others feeling guilty, condemned, and unloved by Jesus because they weren't healed or delivered. We have a miracle working Lord who desires all His children to be healed and set free, but we must always remember Jesus' ways are higher than ours. Continue to seek deliverance, healing, even miracles in your life. Never allow the enemy to steal your desire to praise the Lord as we continue to go through unfortunate things in our lives.

Luke 11:28 *But he said, Yea rather, <u>blessed are they that bear the word of God, and keep it.</u>*

In **Luke 11:24-26**, Jesus was illustrating an unfortunate human tendency that many of us have. We often want to reform to remove sin from our lives, but this resolve doesn't last long. If we get emptied of the evil in our life, then we must be filled with the power of the Holy Spirit to accomplish God's purposes in our lives. **<u>Stay in the Word of God, and fill the empty places!</u>**

What is Fear?

There are so many fears or phobias that man has. The word phobia according to *Webster's Dictionary* is an exaggerated, inexplicable, and illogical fear of a particular object or class of objects. Fear is a feeling of anxiety and agitation caused by the presence or nearness of danger, evil, pain, etc. Timidity, dread, terror, fright, apprehension, or uneasiness are all states of fear. To fear is to expect with misgiving, suspect, or to be doubtful.

Sometimes these phobias enter us as young children. Some are passed down through generations, and some we pick up as adults. Some fears come upon us because we are violated and sinned against. In whatever way these fears or phobias originated, they are very real to people. When we get near the thing that causes us fear, we react.

I have a fear of lizards. I know this seems stupid, but where I grew up in West Texas there were lots of lizards. It seemed like everywhere I walked or played... there they were! These ugly little creatures! I remember one time as a teenager, when I backed my car out of the garage, I ran over the tail of a lizard. For days that lizard stalked me. He was always there when I would leave or return to my home. Have you ever noticed that if you don't like something, you're the one who always notices that thing? I am always seeing lizards before anyone else. Why Lord? Why?

There are <u>so</u> many phobias. For just about anything you can identify, someone will have a fear about it. We have all heard about the fear of heights, darkness, and spiders. What about a fear of failure or the bogeyman? Do you know that some people have *caligynephobia*? This is the fear of beautiful women. Have you heard of *arachibutyrophobia*? This is hilarious! It is the fear of peanut butter sticking to the roof of your mouth. I say, "Yes and amen to that one." If you need one for the church you attend, how about this phobia? If you are really bored with the sermon and need an excuse to leave, you can say you have *homilophobia*. This phobia is the fear of sermons. (Don't tell your preacher I told you!) The list of identified phobias fills page after page. There are so many, it is hard to count them all.

How do we get rid of fear? Scripture gives us the key. When a thought enters our mind, at that moment we have the ability to cast down every vain imagination or react to it. People with a fear believe they are really in danger. Even though the phobias feel so powerful, we, the children of God, can be rid of them. Don't let Satan steal your joy, your peace, or your very walk with God by keeping you in bondage to fear. Paul states in **2 Timothy 1:7,**

2 Timothy 1:7 *For God hath not given us the spirit of fear; but of power, and of love, and of a sound mind.*

If we allow phobias to be in our mind, how can our mind be sound? <u>It can't</u>.

The way to freedom is through prayer, sometimes fasting, and having someone pray with us to cast the demon out. Oh, but Leslie, a Christian can't have a demon. Oh, really? We aren't a sinless bunch of people. We need to strive daily to be cleansed from all unrighteousness. We allow the enemy to come in or not. I have seen demons cast out of people, yes, believers in the

Lord Jesus Christ many times. Why do you think the church is full of fornicators, adulterers, sodomites, liars and drug abusers, just to name a few? The reason is because believers have allowed the enemy to come into their houses.

> **Matthew 12:25-29 *And Jesus knew their thoughts, and said unto them, Every kingdom divided against itself is brought to desolation; and every city or house divided against itself shall not stand: And if Satan cast out Satan, he is divided against himself; how shall then his kingdom stand? And if I by Beelzebub cast out devils, by whom do your children cast them out? therefore they shall be your judges. But if I cast out devils by the Spirit of God, then the kingdom of God is come unto you. Or else how can one enter into a strong man's house, and spoil his goods, except he first bind the strong man? and then he will spoil his house.***

According to these verses, **Satan cannot cast himself out. He, Satan cannot be divided against himself.** If this is the case, then how can the strong man be Satan? Obviously, this doesn't make sense. Satan is <u>not</u> the strong man. Satan and his workers of darkness want to bind you up. The only way that he can do this is if you allow him to. The strong man is you and me. The strong refers to man.

This means no one can enter into another man's body, (his temple)...our temple *"except he first bind the strong man."* "He" in this Scripture is referring to Satan. The only way he can spoil someone's house is first to bind and tie the person up. <u>Satan wants to take you into captivity. He wants to put you in bondage.</u> When evil is lurking in your mind, you either have the authority to rebuke and command the evil thought to go or you can give into it and go through with the sin you are being tempted with.

As stated in the previous chapter, most principles in the Bible involve either being bound or loosed. In other words, we can stay in darkness and be bound up by unforgiveness, bitterness, being out of control...or we can be free and loosed from these bondages. It's up to us.

Matthew 12:33-37 <u>***Either make the tree good, and his fruit good; or else make the tree corrupt, and his fruit corrupt; for the tree is known by his fruit.***</u> *O generation of vipers, how can ye, being evil, speak good things? for out of the abundance of the heart the mouth speaketh. A good man out of the good treasure of the heart bringeth forth good things: and an evil man out of the evil treasure bringeth forth evil things. But I say unto you, That every idle word that men shall speak, they shall give account thereof in the day of judgment. For by thy words thou shalt be justified, and by thy word thou shalt be condemned.*

How Strong are you?

Who is stronger than we are? The one who is stronger is the temptation that overcomes you. This is why when you open the door of your house through unrighteousness, the enemy comes into destroy you. Satan wants to put you into captivity. If, at the moment of temptation you don't resist and flee from it, Jesus says you will be in a worse state than you were before. He goes on to say that blessed are they that hear the Word of God, and keep it.

Once we are free, we are to continue to persevere and strive to be clean.
The only way that Satan can have his demons enter in again is if he finds that the person is empty. This is why it is important to stay in the Word of God, especially after a deliverance has taken place. You must fill the void with the Word of God. Don't allow fear to overtake you. No matter how silly or serious
the fear is, **<u>you can overcome!</u>**

Quotes of Well Known People

Franklin D. Roosevelt said, "The only thing we have to fear is fear itself."
Another quote from Mohandas K. Gandhi is, "There would be no one to

frighten you if you refused to be afraid."

One of my favorite quotes is, "Fear is that little darkroom where negatives are developed."

Jesus, The Perfect Love

If you think about some of your fears or phobias, when did they develop in your mind and become bigger than life? I have a friend who for a long time had a fear of doctors. The reason being is when he was a young boy his mom and a nurse held him down, against his will, to give him a shot. Negative thoughts entered this young boy's mind and continued to grow and cloud his thoughts until he was an adult. Through prayer, we finally recognized where the fear began. Only then was this friend able to release the fear.

Sometimes the fear is so deep-rooted we can't even pinpoint its origin. It could come from other children teasing you, a brother or sister, or even mom and dad about something you were afraid of. Wherever it began is where the authority of Jesus Name needs to be applied. Seek the Lord and He will set you free. Get the facts first, THEN panic! Just kidding. We never need to panic; we need to be free.

Remember,
Jesus is our perfect love which casteth out **all** fear!

1 John 4:18 *__There is no fear in love; but perfect love casteth out fear:__ because fear hath torment. He that feareth is not made perfect in love.*

The only fear we should have is a reverential fear of the Lord. **Proverbs 1:7** it says, *"The fear of the Lord is the beginning of knowledge."* **Psalms 111:10** we are told that the fear of the Lord is the beginning of wisdom. This is a sense of awe and reverence for the Lord and is different from man's fears.

Remember, *though I walk through the valley of the shadow of death, I will fear no evil: for **thou art with me!*** Can a shadow hurt you? No! It's not real. A shadow just lurks around and is powerless. Fear no evil, for the Lord thy God is with you.

> **Psalms 23:4** *Yea, though I walk through the valley of the shadow of death, I will fear no evil: for thou art with me; thy rod and thy staff they comfort me.*

How Do I Stay Free?

Remember in order to be free, you must desire that freedom. To stay free, you must fill the void (your clean house) with the Word of God.

If someone doesn't truly want to be rid of the demons in their life, they are then giving permission to the powers of darkness to stay.

We cannot serve two masters. We need to decide which one we are going to serve. Do not serve fear, because that will only keep you in bondage.

Which do you choose? Life or death? These are in the power of the tongue. (**Proverbs 18:21**).

> **Proverbs 18:21** *Death and life are in the power of the tongue: and they that love it shall eat the fruit thereof.*

Remember, binding and loosing is something we must be aware of and apply the truth daily. Everything we do either puts us in bondage (where we are bound up) or results in us being free and loosed from the law of sin and death.

We have the authority to bind the flesh of someone's tongue. We don't have the authority to bind a demon.

Psalms 149:8 *To bind their kings with chains, and their nobles with fetters of iron;*

However, we need to be cautious about binding and loosing. We as Christians go about binding this, loosing that, and looking for demons in everybody and everything. Even though we have authority to bind somone's flesh, is this something we really want to do? Remember, it is no different than putting a curse on someone. The only time I would bind the tongue of a person is if they are cursing me.

Over the years of ministry, my husband and I have received a few letters filled with curses. I remember one in particular. They cursed us to death, not only us physically, but our ministry also. This person's tongue needed to be tied up. Once we send a curse to someone (another Christian), the prayers are still being answered. We need to be very cautious about being so free to bind up others. Is putting somone in bondage what you really want to do? Is it a flesh response on your part? The Lord will caution us to be careful in our given authority. Let's not use the authority Jesus gave to His children to do more harm to each other. For someone to be free they must desire to be free, or the evil spirits will come into the swept, clean house seven times worse. Recognize the power and authority you have in the Name of Jesus, but use it with the reverential fear of the Lord.

The Full Armor of God

Memorize this prayer. Teach your children to pray no matter what their age is.

Father, I come to You in the Name of Jesus. I ask forgiveness for my sins. I remit the sins of my forefathers and ask that no curse will be put to my charge. I remit the sins from the tenth generation back, or as far back as need be. I also declare that no curse will be in my generation or further generations to come.

I put on my full armor of God; the helmet of salvation, the breastplate of righteousness, the belt of truth around my loins, and the shield of faith. I have the sword of the Spirit and my feet are shod with the gospel of peace. I am standing on your Word, the Word of God.

I plead the Blood of Jesus over my spirit, soul, and body—over my health, mind, conscious, subconscious, and subliminal areas. I plead the Blood of Jesus over my family members and loved ones. I plead the Blood of Jesus over our property and ministry. All that you have placed in my hands and care, I plead Your Blood of protection over us.

I ask Lord of hosts to place your ministering and guardian angels around about me and my family today. Cleanse us from all unrighteousness, and hear our prayer.

In Jesus' Name, Amen.

This simple prayer is a must for us as Christians today.

<u>DO NOT LEAVE HOME WITHOUT IT!</u>

The Armor of God

Ephesians 6:10-18 Finally, my brethren, be strong in the Lord, and in the power of his might. Put on the whole armour of God, that ye may be able to stand against the wiles of the devil. For we wrestle not against flesh and blood, but against principalities, against powers, against the rulers of the darkness of this world, against spiritual wickedness in high places. Wherefore take unto you the whole armour of God, that ye may be able to withstand in the evil day, and having done all, to stand. Stand therefore, having your [1] loins girt about with truth, and having on [2] the breastplate of righteousness; [3] And your feet shod with the preparation of the gospel of peace; Above all, taking [4] the shield of faith, wherewith ye shall be

able to quench all the fiery darts of the wicked. And take [5] the helmet of salvation, and [6] the sword of the Spirit, which is the word of God: [7] Praying always with all prayer and supplication in the Spirit, and watching thereunto with all perseverance and supplication for all saints;

Chapter 5

Steps to Remember

A: Ask forgiveness of sins. Include sins of your forefathers. Ask the Lord to cleanse you from all unrighteousness.

B: Full Armor of God:

1. Helmet of salvation
2. Breastplate of Righteousness

3. Loins girded about by Truth
4. Shield of Faith

5. Sword of the Spirit
6. Feet shod with the Gospel of Peace

7. Standing on the Word, the Word of God

C: Plead the Blood of Jesus over your:

1. Spirit
2. Soul
3. Body
4. Health
5. Mind
6. Conscious
7. Subconscious
8. Subliminal areas
9. Family members and loved ones
10. Property
11. Ministry
12. Whatever God has given you.

D: Ask for the Lord's angels to be in charge over you and your family.

Remember,

We can do **all** things in Christ, which strengthens us! We are overcomers and fear cannot hold us back from doing the work of the Lord.

Be blessed!

Help Me! I'm All Tied Up!

Summary

This book is a resource for you to study. My prayer is that it will kindle desire in your heart to further study the truth of God's Word. My desire and goal is to give you Biblical truths and reveal the keys to the kingdom of heaven.

The most important thing you must always remember is that we are more than conquerors in Christ Jesus. He is a faithful God and desires that His children be free. You <u>can</u> be an overcomer. Don't become so consumed with the things pertaining to the devil and demons. Remember to focus on the things and Spirits of God. He desires that His children <u>walk</u> in holiness and righteousness.

A word of caution–always remember to put on your full armor of God, plead the Blood of Jesus over you and your family, and place the Lord's angels round about you daily and most certainly before praying for others.

We learn from experience. I want to tell you of an event that took place in my life so that you will hopefully learn and grow in the Lord from my mistakes and lessons learned.

It was April, 1990. My family had just moved from Lawrence, Kansas to Omaha, Nebraska. The day we were moving into our new home, Stan had a prior obligation that he had to fulfill. He wouldn't be there to help me unpack and move into our new home. Stan was going to drive to Kansas to pick up Dumitru Duduman. Dumitru was going to speak in Kansas, Missouri, and Nebraska for about two weeks.

Dumitru was coming to visit us in our new home in less than 24 hours of our moving in. Dumitru Duduman was a prophet of God, sent to America to warn the Church about things the Lord had shown him. He was a mighty man of God who served and loved the Lord most of his life.

I was excited about Dumitru coming to our home, but I was also overwhelmed. I wanted so much for our home to be in perfect order. This included having sheets on the beds, pictures on the walls, towels and curtains hung up...everything in its place. If you have ever moved, you will understand that this was a great undertaking for one person to accomplish. Even so, I was determined to meet this challenge.

As I was emptying boxes, putting things away and washing, I would pray for whomever came to my mind. After several hours of praying, I found that I was very weak, tired, exhausted, overwhelmed, feeling sick and not able to continue. I was so upset that I laid on my bed and began to cry out to the Lord. "Lord, what is wrong? I need to have strength to get this job done. Help me!"

A short time after I said that prayer, the phone rang. It was Stan. Stan said, "Leslie, I don't understand this, but I just picked up Dumitru Duduman. He said I was to call you right away. I was to tell you that the reason you are so weak and feeling sick is because you did not pray for yourself first, and put on your full armor of God before you began to pray for all those people. Their sins are coming back on you because you do not have your protection on." Stan further said, "Does that mean anything to you?" I began to cry profusely and said, "Yes, that speaks to me. I know better! I can't believe that I forgot to put on my full armor and plead the Blood of Jesus over me."

This was an incredibly significant lesson the Lord wanted me to learn so that I would definitely recognize the importance of memorizing and daily praying the prayer of protection.

Remember, as you are delivered from any demonic strongholds in your life, it can either be a temporary thing or a life-changing experience. You must fill the void with the Word of God and desire to stay clean and pure. You must fill the temple of the Holy Spirit constantly. If you neglect this part of the deliverance, then the powers of darkness and the evil principalities will have permission to come back in, worse than before.

Remember,
Choose This Day Whom You Will Serve!

Deuteronomy 30:19 *I call heaven and earth to record this day against you, that <u>I have set before you life and death, blessing and cursing: therefore choose life</u>, that both thou and thy seed may live:*

Joshua 24:15 *And if it seem evil unto you to serve the LORD, <u>choose you this day whom ye will serve</u>; whether the gods which your fathers served that were on the other side of the flood, or the gods of the Amorites, in whose land ye dwell: <u>but as for me and my house, we will serve the LORD.</u>*

Help Me! I'm All Tied Up!

About The Author

Leslie Johnson is Director and Founder of the Women's Conference "*The Perfect Touch*". She is also the Co-founder of *The Power of Jesus Crusades* which are held monthly all across America.

Leslie teaches about intercession, praise and worship. She ministers in and demonstrates the power of Jesus. Leslie has been involved in ministry for over 17 years and was formally ordained on May 7, 2000.

Since then, God has directed her to write books pertaining to what God has done in her life. Leslie is in great demand as a speaker at conferences, seminars, and intercessory groups across the globe. She walks in the anointing of the Holy Spirit and is in the office of prophet.

Leslie's deepest desire is to see God's people set free, delivered, and able to walk in holiness and righteousness.

Additional copies of
Help Me!
I'm All Tied Up!
Binding and Loosing:
Scriptural Truth
are available for $7

Also by Leslie Johnson:

*The Perfect Touch...Responding to
the Voice of the Lord*

*Crown of Glory: Receiving the
Lord's Blessings by Becoming
an Overcomer*

Help Me!
I'm All Tied Up!
Binding and Loosing:
Scriptural Truth

This book reveals the scriptural truths about binding and loosing. You will have scriptural references of the evil spirits and the Spirits of God.

A revelation knowledge will be imparted to you as you begin to see the truth of God's Word. This book will answer questions about what binding and loosing is regarding. It also reveals who is the "strong man" is in the Scriptures. You will have a step-by-step formula for the prayer of protection.

This is a must-read book for all Christians. Jesus paid the price for us to be free from all oppression, depression and possession of evil. Jesus came to set the captives free.

Help Me! I'm All Tied Up! **Binding and Loosing: Scriptural Truth,** will show you the keys to the Kingdom of Heaven as they are unveiled and revealed.

Leslie Johnson
The Prophecy Club®
P. O. Box 750234
Topeka, KS 66675

785-266-1112

Other Works
by Leslie Johnson

THE PERFECT TOUCH...
RESPONDING TO THE VOICE OF THE LORD

Leslie Johnson shows you how God is speaking to His children all the time. You will learn how to hear and recognize the voice of the Lord. It also shows you what God is doing regarding; miracles, healing, prophecy and intercession. It will teach you to become more Christlike. You will begin to see God speaking to you in many ways after reading this book—a real blessing! The comments coming in are, "It is an awesome book," and "Leslie really hears from God."

Order #: TOUCH
Gift of $12

PERFECT TOUCH
WOMEN'S CONFERENCE

Features Leslie Johnson and Mary Gene Stephens. Learn how to successfully raise your sons, understand your husband, and cope with a male boss and men in general—in a Biblical manner. A woman came up to me after the conference and said, "I could have saved two marriages if I would have had this information!" Information becomes knowledge, knowledge is power, and power is turned into wisdom when used correctly and lovingly. The whole conference was packed with humor, fun and information such as: fashion do's and don'ts; nutritional facts; skin care; hair care; nail, hand and foot care. Not only did women receive practical advice, but *The Perfect Touch* from the Lord. If laughter and a merry heart heals, everyone in the whole place was healed!

Order #: WOMEN
Gift of $20

CROWN OF GLORY

This book will teach every individual how to become an overcomer. We all face the challenge or satanic influence, as well as fleshly desires. Learn what the Word of God says needs to be done to receive the crowns from the Lord; also, what needs to be accomplished in our Christian, God-given walk with the Lord. This book answers questions regarding the different crowns mentioned in the Bible and what their significance is. It explains what crowns are available for us now and what crowns we will earn at Christ's appearing. Learn what each crown represents, and why it is important to live a righteous and holy life.

Order #: CROWN
Gift of $12

ADVANCED SPIRITUAL WARFARE

Features a combination of Henry Gruver and Leslie Johnson. If you want to understand how to get the victory in the spirit, so you have the victory in the natural, this is for you. Ten, 90-minute tapes.

Order #: SPIRITUAL A
Gift of $35

To order write to: The Prophecy Club® P. O. Box 750234, Topeka, KS 66675
with payment or fax: (785) 266-6200
Call (785) 266-1112 to order by phone.
Please make all donation checks and money orders payable to: The Prophecy Club®

Additional Picks

DANIEL FOR THE TWENTY-FIRST CENTURY VIDEO

Stan Johnson, Founder of The Prophecy Club®, walks you through Daniel. The primary objective of Daniel is to show us who the Antichrist is; what nation he comes from, how to recognize him, what his personality is and how he rises to power in Iraq; his two attacks on Egypt; one attack on Israel to his fall at Armageddon. You must understand Daniel, as it is the central key to understanding Revelation. His is very encouraging news on how Jesus will protect his own in the trouble ahead. 2 hrs. 40 min.

Video Order #: DANIEL   Gift of $30

JEZEBEL vs. ELIJAH BOOK/VIDEO

Dr. Bree M. Keyton, TH.D., D.C.E. explains how the spirit of Jezebel is alive and wreaking havoc, leading Christians into idolatry, perversion, and promoting her religion of self. Jezebel, the master deceiver and false prophet, turns her uninformed followers into eunuchs and zombies while destroying the true prophets of God. Will you be able to recognize and resist?

Book Order #: JEZEBEL BK   Gift of $17

Video Order #: JEZEBEL V   Gift of $30

NEW AGE BIBLE VERSIONS BOOK/VIDEO

Gale Riplinger's exhaustive six-year collation of new Bible versions, their underlying Greek manuscripts, editions, and editors is culminated by this video. It objectively and methodically documents the hidden alliance between new versions and the New Age Movement's One World Religion. The emerging new Christianity–with its substitution of riches for righteousness, a crown for a cross, and an imitation for a new creation–is shown to be a direct result of the wording in new versions. Documented are the thousands of words, verses, and doctrines by which new versions will prepare the apostate churches of these last days to accept the religion of the Antichrist–even his mark. The Greek manuscripts, critical editions, lexicons and dictionaries behind the new versions are examined; revealing their occult origins, contents, and yet to be-released material–a blueprint for the Antichrist's One World Religion and government. Gale exposes new version editors–in agreement with Luciferians, occultists, and New Age philosophy–in mental institutions, séance parlors, prison cells, and court rooms for heresy trials, and most shocking of all. denying that salvation is through faith in Jesus Christ. Five editors have lost their ability to speak.

Book Order #: BIBLE   Gift of $20

Video Order #: BIBLE V   Gift of $30

REVELATION FOR THE TWENTY-FIRST CENTURY VIDEO

Taught by Stan Johnson, Founder of The Prophecy Club®, walks you through Revelation. Perhaps for the first time you will understand Revelation. See when the Mark of the Beast takes place; when the 144,000 are sealed; and where America is in prophecy and when she is destroyed; when Jesus returns and what happens when He does. Understand whether the seven seals/trumpets/vials are fulfilled consecutively or simultaneously. 2 hrs. 40 min.

Order #: REVELATION   Gift of $30